DIVORCE YOUR DEBT

A Spiritual Journey from
S.E.L.F. Debt to Deliverance

DIVORCE YOUR DEBT

A Spiritual Journey from
S.E.L.F. Debt to Deliverance

By
Terrence and
Marlene Trimuel

Divorce Your Debt
www.DivorceYourDebt.net

Divorce Your Debt
A Spiritual Journey from S.E.L.F. Debt to Deliverance
divorcedebt@gmail.com
www.divorceyourdebt.net

10 9 8 7 6 5 4 3 2
First Edition 2015
Printed in the United States of America

ISBN: 978-0-9909348-3-7

Table of Contents

Foreword

This is what the Lord says: "Was your mother sent away because I divorced her? Did I sell you as slaves to my creditors? No, you were sold because of your sins."
Isaiah 50:1 (NLT)

Sin is the evil that causes us to enter into toxic and unhealthy relationships in our lives. Life itself is lived by and through the relationships we have with everything around us. How we relate to everything around us determines the quality of our lives and the level of fulfillment we experience, also.

Sin, unfortunately, comes about when we stray away from God's set commands and standards for our lives and decide to disobey Him. As we see in Isaiah 50:1 above, the Lord is making a very powerful point to His people who have gone astray. God is simply stating that He is not responsible for the depraved condition of bondage that we find ourselves in; we sell ourselves into bondage because of our relationship with sin. We willfully divorce Him and dismiss Him from our daily lives, when we really should be divorcing our debt of sin and bondage.

We all were created with the gift of free will and have the ability to make choices for our lives. In our modern world, we are constantly encouraged to live our lives solely to satisfy ourselves. We are encouraged to go where we want to go, say what we want to say, live as we want to live, and drink, eat, party, and celebrate undisciplined lifestyles. Rarely do we see a true commitment to live as God has commanded us, and rarely do we see people wanting to truly please Him.

The Bible says that without faith it is impossible to please God. It also teaches us that those who live in sinful lifestyles cannot inherit the kingdom of God. This is not only an issue among unbelievers, but this has become a very serious crisis among the faith community as a whole.

The world is ruled by Satan, and all he brings is preplanned destruction for our lives, because he does not want you and me to experience all the power, glory, and peace that God has for us. He has designed a world system of temptation that is so enticing that it intoxicates us with the promises of true pleasure and riches, yet what he never tells you is that his system is designed for one reason and one reason only: to capture your entire life and place you in *bondage*!

We wrote this book to bring forth awareness to our readers about the system that has captured so many of us in its grip.

This system is sin, and it entices us to enter ourselves into extremely toxic relationships. It is designed to tear down our spirit, emotions, lifestyles, and finances—or our SELF as we know it.

If you purchased this book, then you are ready to begin your spiritual journey to free your SELF from debt. We challenge you to deeply search the four key areas of your life that will be discussed in this book so that you can determine the relationships that are neither rewarding nor healthy. We were created to live a life of purpose, and anything or anyone that is contrary to our progress needs to be eliminated.

It is our sincere desire that you will use this book to take an honest look at those things that have you in bondage and that it will provoke you to take action to divorce your debt.

There is no other way for us to experience the greatness God has in store for us other than facing our issues of debt. In other words, we must break free from every relationship with people, places, and things that cause us to become toxic to ourselves and those around us.

The Apostle Paul sums this all up in Romans 6:12–16 below. We challenge you to digest this lesson, and this book, and allow it to fill your life with the wisdom of true deliverance.

> *12. Do not let sin control the way you live; do not give in to sinful desires.*
>
> *13. Do not let any part of your body become an instrument of evil to serve sin. Instead, give yourselves completely to God, for you were dead, but now you have new life. So use your whole body as an instrument to do what is right for the glory of God.*
>
> *14.* ***Sin is no longer your master,*** *for you no longer live under the requirements of the law.* ***Instead, you live under the freedom of God's grace.***
>
> *15. Well then, since God's grace has set us free from*

the law, does that mean we can go on sinning? Of course not!

16. ***Don't you realize that you become the slave of whatever you choose to obey?*** *You can be a slave to sin, which leads to death, or you can choose to obey God, which leads to righteous living.*

Romans 12:12–16 (NLT)

Acknowledgments

We would like to thank God for entrusting us with His vision to write this book, so that His children can be set free from spiritual, emotional, lifestyle, and financial captivity. We would also like to thank our parents: Gammon Trimuel Sr. in his memory, Sarah Trimuel, and Clement and Lanie Mae Luckett; and our children, Terrence Trimuel Jr. (TJ) and Tamera Trimuel.

A sincere thank you to the rest of our family and friends, who began this journey with us years ago and stayed on the battlefield with us until completion, for your prayers, well-wishes, and support. Also, a heartfelt thanks to the ACTS Foundation for their prayers, and a special thanks to Christopher Carswell for his professional review of our work. We are truly blessed and humbled to be surrounded by such loving family members and friends and thank God each day for His unmerited favor.

We would like to also give a special thank you to T. Dwayne Smith and the Teen Train organization for all your encouragement and support throughout this endeavor.

Christ took you ***from debt to deliverance*** in all aspects of your life, and He became your divorce lawyer and judge, forever giving you access to freedom and power through your faith in Him.

INTRODUCTION

The Real Debt Crisis

Have you ever felt as though your life is in a constant state of bondage, and there is no clear way to become free from the debts you owe? Have you diligently tried to find relief from the entanglements of this bondage through various methods, only to find yourself in worse shape than you were before?

So many of us struggle in life, because we are burdened with more debt than we can afford to pay back. When we have too much debt, we lose focus on our purpose in life, and we enter into a dangerous state of denial.

This causes us to escape from reality as well as abandon any sense of accountability for our actions.

During this cycle of denial and abandonment, we unconsciously create uncontrollable debts that lead us into sinful lifestyle choices. The debts we are discussing go far beyond just money. In every major area of our lives, we can get ourselves into more debt than we can handle. Once this occurs, we create unhealthy spiritual, emotional, lifestyle, and financial relationships that become increasingly toxic to our lives. If we continue on this path of SELF destruction, we will no doubt experience a hopelessness that only God can fix.

According to God's Word, He wants each of us to live debt-free, and He wants us to be lenders, not borrowers. This applies to much more than just our financial state of being. It also applies to our spiritual, emotional, and lifestyle well-being. When we find ourselves in a no-win situation as it relates to these key areas, something has to be done. Tough decisions must be made and carried out in order for us to free ourselves from the clutches of despair. The Bible says, "He whom the Son sets free is free indeed," and in order to live free in Christ, you must *divorce your debt*!

So what is *Divorce Your Debt* all about? *Divorce Your Debt* is not just a book or words on a page; it's a guide to wholeness. It's a declaration of independence and a decree to become free from "every weight that so easily besets us." It's a conscious choice to become liberated from the chains, bondage, and traps of the enemy. We all need to divorce or rid ourselves of something in our lives so we can truly follow God's will and please the master. Galatians 5:1 states, "Christ has set us free to live a free life. So take your stand! Never again let anyone put a harness of slavery on you." *Divorce Your Debt* will guide you from debt to deliverance so you can set your SELF free!

God is our ultimate DA—deliverance agent. He sees and knows what we need to be delivered from, even before we can see it within ourselves. The hardest part for most people of today is acknowledging that they need deliverance. The enemy has done his job well by pulling the covers over our eyes and influencing us to believe that we have it all together. However, when we take the time to honestly examine our lifestyles, our circumstances, our finances, our spirituality, and our relationships, we will see that we are in desperate need of deliverance from debt. The question is: Are we willing to go through the process of deliverance by divorcing our debt?

Deliverance is needed in so many aspects of our lives. Just as the children of Israel cried out for deliverance from the bondage they endured for over four hundred years, we all seek to be delivered from the debts and bondage we have found ourselves in even to this day. Even after the children of Israel were delivered from the clutches of bondage, they still found themselves wandering in a wilderness for forty years, because they did not understand or appreciate what God was doing in their lives. We are still like the Israelites were in many ways, even to this day. When we are delivered from a bad habit, situation, or relationship that represents bondage in our lives, we often wander around without clear direction or understanding of what to do next. This leads to us slipping back into bondage over and over again until we learn how to stay "debt-free."

This book was written to help you identify the key areas and situations in your life that represents bondage and debt. The major areas this book focuses on are what we like to call the ***SELF Debt Assessment*** or ***SDA*** for short. **SELF stands for Spiritual, Emotional, Lifestyle, and Financial Debt.** These key areas cover a vast array of the debts we find ourselves struggling with to regain control over our lives. During your SELF Debt Assessment, you will be able to determine who or what is controlling you in your relationships.

We tend to "get married" to unhealthy relationships and stay involved in them for far too long. These unhealthy relationships control us, because we are indebted or obligated to them. Indebted means to place oneself under an obligation. When we are obligated to someone or something, we are being unconsciously controlled. Remember, whatever controls us, rules over us!

Many times, several years will pass before we realize that we have just wasted our time in a relationship that does not work for us. When some people see that their marriage is not working, they make a grueling decision to get a divorce. When a divorce takes place, there is a gut-wrenching process that happens between the people involved. This usually takes time and energy away from those seeking to separate themselves.

Divorce is so difficult because there are so many attachments and soul ties involved. The parties involved have created a collection of memories and things together, they may have produced children, and they have become attached to each other in every aspect. In reality, many divorces occur because the relationships have become toxic. Something has been introduced to the relationship by one or both parties that has compromised the initial covenant or bond established.

Now let's be clear on some things at this point. The authors of this book do not advocate or support divorce unless absolutely necessary from a biblical perspective; nor are the comments in this book intended to promote the concept of matrimonial divorce.

The book, however, is designed to parallel a very common practice in our world today by which marriages are dissolved with being able to dissolve our toxic habits, bad relationships, and bad lifestyle choices in the same manner. These bad relationships and choices take us down a path of life that resembles the debts we owe to our creditors. We become frustrated, agitated and fearful, and when we carry too much debt in our lives, we are distracted from the things God has called us to do.

In the chapters that follow, we will examine the critical areas of the **SELF Debt Assessment** that we must identify and divorce so that God can use us to reflect His excellence and glory. We will highlight the key steps in the *Divorce Your Debt* process and how we liberate our minds, bodies, and souls from the eternal grips of the enemy, Satan. We will also discuss how to maintain our *SELF* health for the future so that we will not slip back into bondage again.

> *We use God's mighty weapons, not worldly weapons, to knock down the strongholds of human reasoning and to destroy false arguments. We destroy every proud obstacle that keeps people from knowing God. We capture their rebellious thoughts and teach them to obey Christ.*
> (2 Corinthians 10:4–5, NLT)

The enemy will use your debt to hold over your head and remind you that you are inadequate to break free from these strongholds alone. He uses obstacles and demonic forces like guilt and shame to control your mind and prevent your breakthroughs from happening. But the one big secret the enemy does not want you and me to know about is the power of our faith in Jesus Christ.

Jesus paid all our debts in advance when He died on the cross at Calvary and rose again on the third day. This means that spiritually, you don't owe this world or the enemy anything! You are free to worship God, and you are free from the bondage that self-condemnation brought to you.

Christ took you *from debt to deliverance* in all aspects of your life, and He became your divorce lawyer and judge, forever giving you access to freedom and power through your faith in Him. The enemy knows that everything he tells you is a lie, as he is the father of lies.

> *...He has always hated the truth, because there is no truth in him. When he lies, it is consistent with his character; for he is a liar and the father of lies.*
>
> (John 8:44 NLT)

All the things he tries to convince you that you must be a slave to are false and deceitful! This includes your past, your mistakes, your bad habits, your old friends, your old lifestyles, your bad choices, everything.

God wants you to free your SELF, and live free in Christ. Divorce your debt!

The enemy knows that once you move past just acknowledging Christ's existence to the level of trusting and believing Him at His word, and when you receive the Holy Spirit, you become debt-free immediately. Understand that there are so many people in the church itself who merely acknowledge Christ's existence and falsely believe that they are saved. Christ requires you to have faith, and faith is not a simple statement made in joining a church, it is *trust in action.*

According to the second chapter of the book of James, your faith must be visible in order to be authentic. In other words, you have to show God and others how your faith works, not just talk about it. For example, if you tell me you have a new watch, and I ask you what time it is, but you tell me your watch is broken, what good is that watch to you or me? The purpose of a watch is to tell us what time it is.

If I mention to you that I need an immediate ride somewhere and you tell me that you have a car, but the car is not working, there really is no purpose in telling me about the car in this situation. The purpose of a car is to provide us with transportation. If the car cannot *get us from one place to another*, then that car is useless and therefore should not be mentioned. This also holds true with our faith. It is designed to help us get from one place to another, and if it cannot, it is useless. Also, just as that car is designed to carry passengers along with you, your faith is designed to help carry others along until they are able to activate their own transportation of faith.

Your authentic faith makes you understand that you have a way out. We have the most precious method of release and relief in our Lord and Savior. This means that you no longer hold yourself in condemnation for the wrong choices and mistakes you've made, nor do you allow guilt, shame, or bad lifestyle habits to continue to keep you in bondage.

The word of God teaches us that He whom the Son sets free is truly free indeed. Jesus is truth, and the word of God says the truth will set you free. Only Jesus can set you free and no one else, so you must activate and live by faith. The Apostle Paul teaches us in Hebrews 10:38 that the just shall live by faith. Faith in Jesus frees us from all debts and bondage, so stop living in them. Live debt-free and clear! Divorce your debt!

God has revealed to us that debt is actually the **DE**vil's **B**est **T**rap, and is manifested in four major categories in our lives: **spiritual debt, emotional debt, lifestyle debt, and financial debt (SELF).**

CHAPTER 1

SELF Debt Assessment

The SELF Debt Assessment was developed as a road map to help you identify and analyze the areas in your life in which you accumulate debt. Debt is such a small word, a four-letter word that has captured the lives of us all in a very big way since the beginning of our existence. Debt, simply defined, is owing repayment on something that someone has loaned to you or paid on your behalf. You are thus in a state of indebtedness, and this is when a relationship of obligation begins.

Debt accumulation can occur in more ways than you have probably ever imagined or thought about. Debt is nothing more than the worst form of bondage. When we consider the thought of debt, we immediately tend to focus strictly on those things that we are financially in debt for—things such as credit cards, loans, mortgages, etc. However, God has revealed to us that debt is actually the **DE**vil's **B**est **T**rap, and is manifested in four major categories in our lives: spiritual debt, emotional debt, lifestyle debt, and financial debt. (SELF). The SELF Debt Assessment is designed to make you aware of the areas that may have your life in a state of bondage. We, the authors, realize, however, that this may be a difficult exercise to complete before you finish reading this book, so please feel free to return to this exercise at the end.

However, we do believe that the questions in the SELF Debt Assessment are very important to keep in your mind as you read this book to set an open and honest atmosphere within yourself.

So with that in mind, the questions that you need to ask yourself in the SELF Debt Assessment are as follows:

SELF DEBT ASSESSMENT

1. To whom and what am I indebted? (List those persons or things that control your life negatively in your spirit, emotions, lifestyle, and finances.)

____

____

____

____

____

____

2. How did I get myself in this debt and bondage in the first place? (Be honest about what you believe led you into this bondage.)

____

____

____

3. What toxic circumstances have developed from my debt? (List the negative results that have come from your toxic debt relationships.)

4. What am I doing right now to free myself from this bondage?

5. Am I allowing fear to stop me from being free?

6. If fear is an issue, what am I afraid of?

7. What am I willing to do to divorce my SELF debt?

8. How will I hold myself accountable for my SELF debt-free commitment?

What did you learn from your SELF Debt Assessment? Did you recognize some things in your life that have taken control over you?

From the time you are born, there is an unseen plan by Satan to lure you into a lifetime of captivity. Captivity is not just capturing you in a physical sense, but it is more about capturing your mind, body, spirit, and finances. You see, Satan figured mankind out a long time ago, and his objective is to get you so caught up in debt that you will never be able to uncover God's purpose, nor your true potential in life. This is because when you are in severe debt, it controls just about every aspect of your life.

Just think about it for a moment. Whenever you have been faced with a major debt or bill that you could not afford to pay, what effect did it have on your time, health, emotions, and decisions? How much mental and physical stress did your debt cause you?

If you are honest with yourself, you will probably admit that when you are in debt, it causes you some sleepless nights and overwhelming frustration, and it probably compels you to do things you would not normally do. The type of debt I'm referring to in this example is merely financial debt. However, the other forms of debt found in the SELF Debt Assessment all work in the very same way.

The enemy is the father of lies, and he works very hard to convince us that we owe our lives to people and things around us. When you allow yourself to be captured by the enemy and held accountable for debts you cannot afford, he gains control over your life and interferes with your relationship with God. It is his goal to keep us entangled in destructive and distractive situations long enough to diminish our worship relationship with our Heavenly Father.

This is his whole objective—to put you in the same misery he feels now that he is an enemy to God. God's love for you and me is so incredible that it makes Satan sick to his evil stomach. Therefore Satan uses spiritual, emotional, lifestyle, and financial debt to destroy our love relationship with our creator.

Spiritual Debt: Satan wants to put your spiritual life in critical condition. He knows that our spirit holds the very essence of God within it, and if he can get us to serve him through evil and sinful living, then he can exercise a certain dominion over us. Look at what Paul had to say about evil:

> *So the trouble is not with the law, for it is spiritual and good. The trouble is with me, for I am all too human, a slave to sin. I don't really understand myself, for I want to do what is right, but I don't do it. Instead, I do what I hate. But if I know that what I am doing is wrong, this shows that I agree that the law is good. So I am not the one doing wrong; it is sin living in me that does it. And I know that nothing good lives in me, that is, in my sinful nature.* I want to do what is right, but I can't. I want to do what is good, but I don't. I don't want to do what is wrong, but I do it anyway. But if I do what I don't want to do, I am not really the one doing wrong; it is sin living in me that does it.*
>
> (Romans 7:14–20 NLT)

I have discovered this principle of life—
that when I want to do what is right, I inevitably
do what is wrong. I love God's law with all my
heart. But there is another power within me*
that is at war with my mind. This power makes
me a slave to the sin that is still within me. Oh,
what a miserable person I am! Who will free me
from this life that is dominated by sin and death?
Thank God! The answer is in Jesus Christ our Lord.
So you see how it is: In my mind I really want to
obey God's law, but because of my sinful
nature I am a slave to sin.
(Romans 7:21–25 NLT)

This explains our human struggle that each of us must fight every day. Many of us want to do good for the Lord at all times, but the nature of our human flesh leads us astray so frequently. We try to live a life that leads us to obedience, peace and joy, yet we open dangerous doors in our lives that lead us to disobedience, debt, and destruction.

The spirit man in all of us is our most precious gift from God and the enemy wants to steal it from the Lord. Since it is difficult to just come to us directly and demand our spirit, Satan uses deceptive and evil tactics to lure us into submission to sin. He knows all too well that if we live in sin long enough, our spirit will be damaged beyond repair, and we will end up just like him. Misery loves company.

We will have a more in-depth conversation about spiritual debt in chapter 3.

Emotional Debt: Satan uses your emotions to coerce you to make deadly life decisions.

When we get caught up in bad relationships and bad circumstances, we often find ourselves making very bad decisions that can be linked to our emotional condition at that time. For example, if we were to find out that someone physically hurt a close family member, particularly one of our children, we could very easily find ourselves in legal trouble for battery or manslaughter, depending on the severity of the act. This is because in a moment like this, our emotions get the best of us, and the enemy uses our anger emotion to react to what we feel at that moment, versus acting on sound wisdom and judgment. Can you recall a time when your anger, sadness, frustration, or other emotions caused you to lose control and make the wrong decision? What was the outcome of that situation? Do you feel it should have been handled differently?

The wise thing to always do when faced with a highly intense and emotional moment is to focus on what is righteous and rational. But unfortunately, the enemy knows exactly how to press our buttons to try to get us to break down and make unwise decisions that can have grave consequences.

One major example of this is the story of Job in the Bible. Most people know this story well and remember how Job was specifically targeted by Satan. Satan made a sort of wager with God that he would get Job to curse God to His face by taking away all the things he was blessed with, including his children, his wealth, and his health. His objective was to make Job's life so immensely miserable and vexed, that Job would lose sight of his relationship with God and make an emotional decision to denounce Him.

Satan even used Job's very own wife to urge him to curse God and die. His so-called friends also turned on him by suggesting that he did something wrong or evil to be punished in such a way. Fortunately for Job, he kept his composure, even within the face of his overflowing emotions of anger, sorrow, anguish, frustration, betrayal, loneliness, and emptiness. Job refused to take the emotional bait of Satan, and he never denounced his love for God, in spite of the tremendous pressure he experienced.

We all have these Job-type moments in our lives each and every day. People and circumstances trigger strong emotions within us, and we have to make critical choices at a moment's notice. These choices often determine our character, our outcome, and they most certainly determine if we fall into emotional debt or bondage.

You see, if we fail to process our emotions properly, we could make a quick emotional decision that will cause us to lose relationships, lose sight of our purpose, our money, our very freedom. Once we find ourselves in these situations, we have to work ten times harder to get out of them. This is how debt of any kind usually works; it's easy to get in it, but so much harder to get out!

We have to learn how to properly identify when our emotions are being pushed to the limit by Satan, and how our faith and prayers have to be activated quickly in those moments. If not, we will no doubt make an emotional transaction that will trap us in his grips of debt and bondage. We will discuss emotional debt in more detail in chapter 4.

Lifestyle Debt: Satan wants you to live according to the world's standards, not God's.

Our lifestyle is extremely important to God. Why? Because God wants our lifestyle to reflect His holiness and righteousness. Our lifestyle is what others look at to see if the light of Christ truly lives within us. Unfortunately, many people, including many believers, think that on the one hand, we can profess our commitment to the Lord, yet on the other hand, we can live in allegiance to the world.

In other words, what happens today is that many of us live a life of sinfulness, yet we proclaim that God is the Head of our lives. The Word clearly states in Matthew 6:24 that we cannot serve two masters; one will be loved, and the other will be hated. It also points out in James 1:8 that we cannot be double-minded, because it creates a constant state of instability within us.

Why is our lifestyle so critically important? It is so important because our lifestyle is a reflection of our beliefs, character, and principles. We live our lives based on what we believe is right and wrong, and if our lifestyle clearly reflects sinfulness on a regular basis, then the enemy knows that we will not be effective at all in fulfilling the purpose God has for us and influencing others around us. You see, people listen to what we do more than to what we say.

When we discuss lifestyle debt, we are referring to the ungodly daily practices that we participate in that cause us to fall under the influence of Satan. For example, some of us may drink alcohol on a social basis or only when we go out on a special occasion. In some cases, the person who drinks on occasion may never encounter any major problems or issues in his or her entire life. However, more often than not, we see people who have opened the door to this particular lifestyle choice of drinking, who find themselves falling into alcoholism, sexual promiscuity, drug abuse, lost opportunities, job losses, isolation, distrust, physical injuries, and even death.

Once Satan can get us to embrace certain dangerous and irresponsible lifestyle choices, he knows he can get us into yet more debt and bondage. Bad lifestyle choices often take us away from our families, friends, and yes, even God Himself. When our lifestyles interfere with our relationship with God, that's when the enemy has us where he wants us. Often when we know we are living sinfully, Satan uses guilt, shame, and condemnation to create distance in our relationship with God. We will tend to avoid praying to God, avoid attending worship services, avoid biblical studies, reject the truth, and justify our sins.

When the enemy has us in this dark place, he makes us believe that we have committed far too much sin for God to ever forgive us, which is a complete lie straight from the pit of hell. The word of God actually teaches us that if we confess our sins, God is faithful and just to forgive us. God's only requirements for us, when we live in a sinful lifestyle, are confession and repentance. Simply put, God wants us to admit to Him the wrong that we are doing and then stop doing it. This is all He requires for our lifestyle debts to be paid in full. If we believe the lies that Satan feeds us regarding our lifestyle, we will remain in a constant state of guilt, shame, procrastination, and unnecessary bondage. So take a look at your lifestyle choices right now, and ask yourself if you are truly living up to God's standards. Are you honestly content with where your lifestyle has positioned you? What things do you need to change right now in order to get closer to God's standards?

Now, we must understand some key things here, also. God does not bless a sinful lifestyle. In other words, when we experience what seem to be "good things" while we are living in a sinful lifestyle, we cannot assume that God is pleased with what we are doing, and therefore we cannot justify staying in that sinful lifestyle.

For example, there are many people who smoke cigarettes regularly. Some say that each time they attempt to stop, they gain too much weight. When they begin smoking again, they say that their weight returns to normal, and therefore it justifies their smoking habit. Well, this is just one example of a lifestyle choice that causes so many of us to pay an extremely high price.

There has been no study ever done on smoking that has ended with a positive result on its effects on the human body. Nicotine is a drug and causes major health problems, including cancer, which leads to death. There is no way that smoking to keep our weight down or our appetites under control is in any way a blessing from God. It cannot be justified at all. This is a trick of the enemy to kill us slowly through the poison of his lies. If he can lure us into a lifestyle that slowly takes away our health, family, friends, and ultimately God, then he wins the battle, and we lose. We have to divorce our lifestyle debts immediately.

Just ask yourself: What lifestyle choices have I made that have caused me to run from God and the truth? What lifestyle choices have I made that have caused my relationships with friends and family to suffer?

After you have asked yourself these questions, ask yourself this final question: Have my lifestyle choices been worth it? If we are truly honest with ourselves, we can almost certainly say no, they have not been worth it. This is why Jesus says in Luke 9:23 that if we are going to follow Him, we must deny ourselves, pick up our cross, and follow Him.

Self-denial is essential to pleasing God. When left to our own rules and lifestyle choices, we humans mess it up every single time. God sent Jesus to be our most perfect example of holiness, and everything He did was to please His father in heaven. This is what God requires of us—that we put aside our own selfish desires and lifestyles to live according to His will. When we do this, we will never have to live in the bonds of lifestyle debt. Is this a difficult task? Of course it is. We hold on to sinful living so tightly because it is a large part of our nature, and to deny ourselves feels like we are dying inside.

Although we may sometimes feel like we cannot let go of our current lifestyle to live a godly one, just think about how much Jesus had to deny Himself. Christ had to leave His heavenly realm, where His lifestyle was filled with all wisdom, power, glory, and righteousness, to come into a sinful world where He had to be clothed in flesh, treated like a criminal, and ultimately betrayed by mankind, which He served unto death. Why did Jesus go through such a change in His very own life in Heaven? Because He loved us so much that He gave it all up for a time and a season to become a sacrifice for our souls. You see, when we complain about what we have to go through in life, none of our experiences will ever match up to the ultimate sacrifice that our savior made for our salvation. More about our lifestyle debt will be further discussed in chapter 5.

Financial Debt: Satan wants you to love money more than the Master.

Financial debt is something that we all can relate to. It's the reason most people get up every morning to go to work at a job that they may not even like. Debt is what our financial system is built on, and we are conditioned to live in debt from a very early age. There was a time in our past when people would save up to buy something they needed or wanted and would make sure that they owed no one. Well, that all changed in the recent past. Our financial system began using debt to finance everything—homes and cars and even a college education. Now we are well trained to reach for a credit card or a loan application whenever we see something we really cannot afford, but we want to have it anyway.

Financial debt is one of the Satan's best traps for us, because he clearly understands that the more debt we owe others, the more time and energy we will have to spend working to pay it all off. The more time we spend working to pay off our debts, the less time we have to develop the greatness God has placed in all of us.

Financial debt has been the root cause of many broken marriages, broken homes, stress, disease and yes, even death. Many have even committed suicide to escape the unbelievable demands of debt repayment. This is because financial debt is truly modern-day slavery. The Bible says very clearly in Proverbs 22:7 that the rich rule over the poor, and the borrower is a slave to the lender.

When we find ourselves lured into financial debt, we are willfully putting ourselves into bondage, and this bondage will cost us most of our time, relationships, and freedom. This is truly one of his best traps, because he uses our lusts and desires to please ourselves against us. The financial world is not designed to set us free, it's designed to enslave us and to keep the rich free and the poor in bondage.

Just think about how many things you have purchased with some sort of loan or credit line. How long will it take you to pay it all off, and what will be the actual cost of your purchase? Keep in mind that when we have to pay back things we buy on credit, we pay them back with interest, so we always have to pay more than what we borrowed.

Let's break down a few of our normal purchases just to see what it will cost us to get out of financial bondage:

1. House purchase: $100,000 (in today's dollars) at 7 percent interest for thirty years of payments will cost you approximately $239,511.

2. Car Loan: $20,000 at 7 percent interest for five years of payments will cost you approximately $23,760.

3. Student Loans: $25,000 at 3 percent interest rate for ten years of payments will cost you approximately $28,968

Summary: $145,000 total money borrowed,
$292,239 total money owed,
$147,239 in interest payments,
over thirty years of payments to make.

As we can see, financial debt can cause us to pay more than we borrowed, and it will make us work to pay off these debts for well over thirty years of our lives.

Sounds like slavery to me! That's exactly the position the enemy wants us all in—enslaved by our financial choices. We must learn to divorce our debt accumulation habits and seek to make wise financial decisions based on what we really can afford. If we must go into a debt situation, we should certainly seek to put ourselves in position to pay it off as quickly as possible.

If we allow ourselves to be brought under financial demands that we cannot truly afford to handle, we find ourselves imprisoned by stress, physical ailments, and potentially a sense of hopelessness. When we look at all of these debts combined, we can see that a divorce is necessary to rid ourselves of the bondage of the enemy. As you read this book, try to be as honest with yourself as possible and identify the areas in which debt has impacted your life. We all need to have our own debt-to-deliverance experience, and this book should be used as a guide to assist you in taking the necessary steps to become "free indeed."

Whenever we find ourselves drowning in debt, we automatically look for ways to get out of it—deliverance by God to cancel the debts or means by which we can pay them off. Deliverance is the process or act of being taken out of a bad situation to a better one. It can also be described as being taken from trouble to triumph. In either description, we find that when we are in debt, we want this deliverance to take place immediately. The purpose of this book is to put things in perspective with respect to identifying the four different categories of debt, and to show us how we can use this understanding to set the stage for our deliverance to manifest.

The authors of this book have been given this assignment as a ministry that has to be shared and taught. We have ourselves endured a great deal of challenges with debt, in all the categories mentioned earlier, so this has become a personal mission for us.

We defile our lives with the decisions we make, and the things we find ourselves unconsciously "married" to will, in many ways, destroy us.

CHAPTER 2

Until Death Do Us Part

According to the Bible, marriage is a permanent covenant relationship between a man and a woman. Marriage is also a human reflection of God's spiritual relationship with mankind. God seeks to be the husbandman of every human being and commands each of us to have no other God before Him. God takes marriage very seriously and expects us to as well. Before marriage occurs, there is usually a process of dating or, as the old school would say, "courting." This process allows each person to get to know the other and find out if the relationship is a good fit.

If the process is done properly, or in other words, approached with the wisdom of God, the relationship will flourish and become an earthly example of our commitment and union with our Father in Heaven. A good marriage involves love, faithfulness, commitment, integrity, respect, submission, peace, consummation, gentleness, spiritual fulfillment, and yes, financial resources.

If these things are not present in a marriage, then it is usually doomed to fail. Not because the marriage in and of itself fails, but because the parties involved often allow their selfish desires and influences to kick in and take control. Many marriages fail simply because one or both parties have left God out of the equation and neglected to allow Him to do His job as our ultimate husbandman. If we allow God to lead us in our marriage, then He will keep it together and let no man put it asunder.

If both parties are not fully committed to ensuring the success of the marriage, then divorce becomes inevitable. The lawyers are called in, legal papers are drawn up, tough decisions are made, court dates are set, arguments on both sides take place, money is spent, a divorce decree is established, and finally the legal dissolution occurs.

Most people feel a sense of relief once this process is over, and they are able to move on with the next chapter of their lives. However, what some people learn later on is that if they had allowed themselves to approach the marriage in a different way, it might have actually worked out. Many find out later on in life that they were actually the bigger problem in the marriage, not their former spouse, but it is too late to recapture what has been lost, in most cases.

Again, the authors of this book are not advocates for divorce unless it is under the rules that the Bible clearly points out in Matthew 19. In this chapter, Jesus points out that divorce was never intended to happen according to God's expectations. Moses allowed it to happen because of the "hardness of the hearts" of mankind. But Jesus did say that the only legitimate basis for divorce is infidelity.

Infidelity or adultery is something that completely violates the covenant between a man and his wife, and God apparently allows the divorce to take place. Infidelity causes distress, depression, distrust, distraction, anger, guilt, shame, violence, lack of peace, lack of focus, bitterness, marital contamination, and yes, even death. Yes, infidelity has caused death to occur in many instances, either because of the desire for revenge or the contraction of disease from a defiled spouse. No wonder God allows divorce in cases such as this. He does not want us involved in any relationship that can bring us as His children to death or destruction.

What we must now understand from all of this is that a good marriage is a relationship built on mutual love, trust, and respect for one another. This kind of love, trust, and respect does not create a sense of bondage and slavery but should create a sense of excitement, safety, comfort, and peace.

Now that we have discussed the marriage relationship between two people, let's examine the nonhuman marriage we find ourselves involved in. This, of course, is our marriage to our debt. Why do we discuss this kind of relationship in terms of a marriage? Well what we, the authors, have learned in our lives is that most people tend to stay more committed to their relationships with their spiritual, emotional, lifestyle, and financial debts than they ever do to their human marital relationships.

For some strange reason, we tend to hold on more tightly to those things that bring us harm and destruction over time, and we push away those things that bring us joy, freedom, and peace. This is why we use the institution of marriage as a metaphor for the relationships we establish with our debts—many of us stay engulfed in toxic debt relationships and bondage until death do us part.

In other words, many of our spirits, emotions, lifestyles, and finances end up in a toxic spiral of debt that we can never satisfy unless we divorce it altogether. We defile our lives with the decisions we make, and the things we find ourselves unconsciously "married" to will, in many ways, destroy us.

We tend to get so used to struggle and dysfunction that we ignore many opportunities to free ourselves from bondage and SELF debt. So naturally, if we compare our debt relationships with marriage, then it's only logical to compare our breaking free from these debts with divorce.

Divorce is something that has affected all of us in some way, either personally or through family members or friends. People talk about divorce all the time in life, but rarely do we ever hear people discussing breaking up with their toxic SELF debt.

It is now time for this discussion to be undertaken so we can all take an honest look at ourselves and realize that we have some extremely dangerous relationships within our spirits, emotions, lifestyles, and finances.

It is time to pull the cover back and truly expose the plots, plans, and schemes of the enemy to lure us into bondage and enslavement.

Are you willing to take this journey and be honest with yourself? Do you want to be set free from your SELF debts?

I believe you do, or you wouldn't be reading this book, so let's continue to press forward and unearth the SELF debt issues we all face.

The mind is the ultimate gatekeeper to
the spirit, and it filters out what is
allowed to come into this very
critical part of our existence.

CHAPTER 3

Spiritual Debt

Spiritual debt is the most critical of the four areas. This is because the condition of your spirit determines the decisions you make in all aspects of your life. Your spirit is what the enemy, Satan, wants to affect the most. Satan wants your mind, body, and spirit to be subject to him alone. He wants you as his personal slave, and he wants you to believe you must live in sin in order to truly live a good and fun life. In other words, he wants the "mortgage" on your spirit. The word mortgage actually means "death pledge" and when a bank issues you a mortgage, they are possibly communicating that they expect you to "die" trying to pay it off! This is the same desire that the enemy has for our spirit. He wants us to be artificially indebted to him and never come to the full knowledge of the one weapon we have to destroy his stronghold on us.

That weapon is none other than the faith in the name and the blood of Jesus Christ.

He cannot get to your spirit easily unless he comes through your mind first. The mind is the ultimate gatekeeper to the spirit, and it filters out what is allowed to come into this very critical part of our existence. Satan uses tactics such as temptation and lust to entice you and seduce your spirit into violating God's commands. He will set you up to commit acts of fornication and overall defilement in order to get your spirit to submit to his authority. Once he is successful with gaining entry, he will wreak havoc on your spirit as he manipulates you into doing his will. The key to him is that he does not come to you with a long tail, red horns, and a pitchfork. No, that would be too obvious. Instead Satan comes to you in the form of a close family member or friend; a trusted doctor or lawyer; a church member or a coworker. He often will create a scenario to draw you in mentally and test your integrity and beliefs.

Let's use an example of an upstanding married man named John. John has three children and a wife of ten years named Michelle. John works very hard as a salesman to provide for his family. John and his wife have both been so busy with raising their children, running their household, and seeing after the needs of other family members that they rarely have time to be intimate with each other. John has brought this up to his wife on numerous occasions, but the conversation seems to come to a stalemate all the time. Michelle feels as though she is a sort of twenty-four-hour servant to her family, her career, and her church. When it's all said and done, she is just too tired and has nothing left for intimacy. John has a coworker named Leslie. Leslie and John have a very cordial friendship and find themselves confiding in each other from time to time about very general, but sometimes private, things.

One night, John and Michelle have a big argument about why he has not had time to repair the broken back door. John uses this opportunity to bring up his extreme frustration about their lack of intimacy. After the argument is over they sleep in separate rooms, and the next day John leaves for work without much conversation. He arrives at work noticeably upset, and the first person he sees is his good friend Leslie. Because John has mentioned to her the issues of intimacy with his wife before, it is easy for him to discuss with her what happened the previous night.

Leslie as always, listens intently and begins to offer him some comfort about the situation. She begins to tell him what a good man he is and that he deserves to be happy. Her words slowly begin to penetrate the core of his subconscious, and he agrees with her assessment. They separate for the rest of the day to conduct their work, and at the end of the day, she reappears to invite him out for drinks with her and a group of other coworkers. John, still upset about the argument he and his wife had the night before, hesitantly agrees to go out with his coworkers, because he is not ready yet to go home and face his wife; he fears another battle might ensue.

Satan has now studied him closely and patiently to find out where he is suffering the most in his marriage. He seeks to expose, exploit, and destroy John by any means necessary, but he knows he cannot just rush in to make the kill. Instead, he will take his time to set John up by developing this relationship with his coworker Leslie.

As the group visits the local bar and grill to unwind, John begins to drink along with his companions for the night, while engaging in more in-depth conversation with Leslie. Leslie rehashes her previous assertion that he deserves to be happy as they continue to toss down margaritas and martinis.

Leslie starts to flirt a little, because the liquor is kicking into high gear, and her deeply rooted desire to get closer to John takes over. John, who has also been tossing down the drinks, lets down his defenses as the liquor kicks in. He begins to flirt back with Leslie, and they decide to leave the bar together to engage in a night of full-blown adultery and fornication.

John returns home late that evening with his desires fulfilled for the moment, but now with the spirit of guilt and shame over the infidelity he participated in. He later tries to cut things off with Leslie, only to discover that she wants more and more of him. Afraid of destroying his ten-year marriage and breaking up his family, John continues to indulge in this illicit affair to keep Leslie from exposing it to his wife. He is now carrying more spiritual debt, because lying, deceit, and lust are in full operation within his spirit.

His spirit has been made a slave or debtor to his indiscretions. Satan patiently observed him and carefully stalked him until he saw an open opportunity to move in for the kill. This is how he works in all of our lives. He uses the weak points in our lives to create spiritual indebtedness. Satan sets traps for us to fall into when we least expect it, and he is a master trap setter. He uses temptations and indulgences such as alcohol, drugs, sex, lust, and other pleasures to weaken our mental defenses, so he can more easily slip in and destroy us.

This example of John being led into spiritual indebtedness is just one example of the many tactics that the enemy attacks us with. Some of us grew up in situations where the enemy used a family member or close family friend to act as a predator in our lives. Many people find themselves being taken advantage of in their early stages of life, which no doubt opens a critical door to the enemy.

For example, when a young child experiences molestation by a trusted family member or friend, Satan uses the evil spirits of confusion, guilt, shame, embarrassment, and defilement to enter into the mind and spirit of that child. Children who have been abused are often threatened to keep their mouths shut and not reveal the dirty truth which creates isolation for that child.

Once Satan has you isolated from those in your life who could actually assist you in getting help and deliverance, then he has you where he wants you—in spiritual bondage and debt. Many people who have been molested and violated, begin to live lifestyles of sexual promiscuity, infidelity, fornication, homosexuality and prostitution, because Satan has convinced them that they are worthless and that God is disgusted by the person that they have become. When Satan has opened up the door through which he takes away our innocence and makes us feel dirty, worthless, and hopeless, that's when he has achieved his ultimate victory of spiritual indebtedness.

The first thing we must do to get out of this state of hopelessness is to identify the problem and realize that we have a way out of any spiritual mess that we get ourselves into. We must recognize that we have entered into "unholy matrimony" with sin and evil and call on our Savior Jesus Christ to help us divorce our spirit from the enemy and enter a new covenant relationship with Christ. When we first recognize that we cannot act as our own lawyer in this divorce, we can then properly turn our situation over to the best lawyer/advocate that ever lived; Attorney and Savior Jesus Christ, JD (justification and deliverance).

Jesus tells us in Matthew 11:28–30, "Come unto me, all ye that labour and are heavy laden, and I will give you rest. Take my yoke upon you, and learn of me; for I am meek and lowly in heart: and ye shall find rest unto your souls. For my yoke is easy, and my burden is light."

When we are bogged down and beaten up by the enemy, we cannot fight him by ourselves. This is why Jesus tells us in Matthew 11 to come to Him, and He will give us rest. In other words, when we give our spiritual debt over to Jesus, He will give us the relief or rest we need. We must then begin to pray to Him for forgiveness, because in the financial world, another word for debt cancellation is forgiveness.

When we pray to God for forgiveness of our spiritual debt, we are essentially asking him to cancel our debt and restore us to a zero balance.

In other words, when we activate our faith in Christ and submit our spiritual debts to Him, He takes them and cancels out everything we thought we owed. He declares us righteous, and we are justified by our faith. The spiritual divorce decree is issued, and we are thus free from the bondage of the evil one. Only Jesus has the power to cancel our spiritual debts. This divorce decree He gives us is a spiritual document of release and authority for us as citizens of His Kingdom to use against the false power of the enemy.

Once He has delivered us from this debt, we are to "seek ye first the Kingdom of God and His righteousness..." in all that we do, which includes studying His word, praying without ceasing, praising Him for what

He has done, and worshiping Him for who He is. We must be careful, by maintaining our relationship with Christ, never again to allow our spirit to enter back into the same indebtedness.

This is extremely important, because the Bible teaches us in Matthew 12 that when an unclean spirit comes out of someone, it will wander around in dry places to seek a resting place. If it cannot find one outside, it will seek to return to that person, and if it finds that person is still empty on the inside, it will bring seven other spirits more evil than it was. This will then make the current condition of that person much worse than it was before the evil spirit was cast out. This means that when Christ breaks the bonds of spiritual indebtedness and issues the enemy the divorce decree, we must immediately get busy serving Him and filling our hearts with righteousness; otherwise, we are doomed to allow ourselves to be bound again and again.

We should seek to help enlighten others by becoming advocates for those who are spiritually in debt. In other words, we need to become DAs, deliverance agents. We, the authors, have made a commitment to become full time DAs for Christ. The DA (deliverance agent) works for the Master to help those who have been enslaved by debt find the permanent relief they need. Our job is to teach and lead others to the Master so that they can file their debt divorce decree by activating their faith. We must help them declare once and for all that debt will no longer rule their lives in any way. The Bible states that we are not to owe any man, and there is no condemnation for those who are in Christ Jesus.

Our emotions can act as mind-altering drugs at times of great stress and chaos.

CHAPTER 4

Emotional Debt

Human beings are emotional creatures by nature. Our emotions are an inseparable part of our makeup and design. We are reflections of God, and God has emotions, so we therefore also have emotions. Emotions are the inner feelings we experience as we face various circumstances in our lives.

For example, we feel great joy and excitement when our children are born. We feel pain and grief when our loved ones die. We feel compassion when we see someone suffering with an illness. We feel anger when someone hurts us or disrespects us. Our emotions are attached to our senses and our conscience.

Many of us make important decisions based primarily on emotions—how we feel at the time. In many cases this is a good thing to do, especially when showing compassion for others who are in need. If we see someone struggling to get out of a bad place in his or her life, God has programmed our emotions to feel compassion so that we will be moved to help them out. God is Love, and this is the ultimate emotion that is supposed to dictate our actions and reactions to life's situations.

As with everything, however, there is a good side to our emotions and a bad side. We are built with other emotions that Satan manipulates in order to get us into the second type of debt, emotional debt. The enemy uses the spirits of fear, anguish, hatred, bitterness, grief, shame, loneliness, rejection, guilt, sorrow, stress, jealousy, and envy to mislead us into making bad life choices. Yes, let's be clear on this point. These are emotions that also can represent evil spirits that are dispatched by Satan. If he can get you to become consumed by these emotional spirits, he can imprison you in emotional bondage and debt.

Satan's tactics began as far back as the Garden of Eden with Eve. He began to tempt Eve by appealing to her emotions, thus setting the stage for all mankind to be in debt to sin. Satan told Eve that the forbidden fruit was actually a good thing to desire. He made her promises that were greatly distorted. He told her that she would become as God, knowing the difference between good and evil. However, Satan failed to mention that by convincing her to partake of the forbidden fruit and by getting Adam to do the same, they would doom mankind to the sentence of death.

In our previous chapter, we discussed how Satan must enter through our minds and use evil strategies to gain access. Well, the biggest weapon he uses to gain access to our minds and ultimately our spirits is our very own emotions.

Our emotions can act as mind-altering drugs at times of great stress and chaos. So many people throughout history, such as Adam and Eve, made life-altering decisions while being intoxicated by their emotions. Intoxication occurs when a foreign substance or an emotion takes over your ability to be alert, aware, and of sound judgment. This goes hand and hand with temptation. Satan uses temptation to get the attention of your emotions and stir them up to a level of intoxication. Once the emotions are under the influence of Satan's temptations, he then tries to convince us to take action in a negative, sinful way.

We must understand and realize that there is a distinct difference between a temptation and a test. Most people unknowingly think of these two distinct realities as interchangeable. However, they operate in two different ways and come from two separate sources.

Tests come from God. A test is designed to bring you closer to the Lord and almost always involves the requirement to sacrifice something to help a cause for someone else. For example, there are times when we are faced with somebody in need who comes to us at an inconvenient time for something that we want for ourselves, such as our last dollar, or our precious time, or something else we cherish. The test usually requires that we either give up some part, or that entire thing, to help the situation of that person. If we do what is right, it brings us closer to God, and we store up treasure in heaven. We have passed the test, and just like in school, we are promoted. In John 15:13, God's word has this to say regarding our sacrifices for each other: "There is no greater love than to lay down one's life for one's friends" (NLT).

Temptations, on the other hand, *always* come from Satan. A temptation is an invitation to commit a sinful act that goes against the will of God. Temptations appeal to the self-centered part that exists in all of us, and they are designed for us to act on something that brings us pleasure or fulfills our own selfish lusts. They are designed to draw us away from God's will by enticing us to do the things that will open the door for the spirits of guilt, shame, condemnation, and many other evils. Temptations never come from God, because God never tempts His people.

James 1:13–15 (NLT) says:

> *13. And remember, when you are being tempted, do not say, "God is tempting me." God is never tempted to do wrong, and he never tempts anyone else.*
>
> *14. Temptation comes from our own desires, which entice us and drag us away.*
>
> *15. These desires give birth to sinful actions. And when sin is allowed to grow, it gives birth to death.*

This is exactly how the enemy gets us messed up in our emotions. He uses temptation as his favorite weapon and attempts to "intoxicate" us to commit sin.

If we are experiencing anger, Satan will convince us to do something about the person or situation that upset us. He will cause our anger to turn into bitterness, and bitterness into rage. After we reach this level in our emotions and become sufficiently intoxicated, he then makes suggestions that enter our mind either through the comments of others or through that wicked, contentious voice that is playing in our heads, telling us to take revenge.

When we are intoxicated, it prohibits us from thinking clearly and soberly. Paul taught us in the book of Titus 2, that we must always be sober minded in all that we do. If we are not sober minded, we risk making decisions that could very well cost us our lives.

In the previous chapter, we discussed the infidelity of John with his coworker Leslie to illustrate how we can become spiritually in debt. Well, the main thing that caused John to follow through on this act of defilement and adultery were his emotions of anger and resentment toward his wife, Michelle, for their lack of intimacy. John was also feeling rejection and loneliness, which Satan counted on to pounce on him during his moment of weakness.

When Satan has you upset, stressed out, and otherwise distracted, that's when he will often introduce extra reinforcements like alcohol and drugs to further weaken your ability to fight off his imminent attack. He is counting on your temporary moments of weakness in the flesh and your desire to change your emotional state of mind, so he can swoop in and do his dirty work.

Oftentimes, when people are upset, they turn to mind-altering substances to "take the edge off." This is usually because many people in our society have become conditioned to being medicated and intoxicated as a means to deal with life issues. When we have physical pain, the first thing we look for is medication. Whether it's a headache, a backache, or some other painful disorder, we tend to reach for a pill or a quick fix to get relief from the pain. The same thing happens when we are hurt emotionally. We tend to turn to the things that we feel will best medicate the pain, which in turn allows the enemy easier access to controlling our emotions.

In our example, John wanted to medicate the pain he was experiencing with his wife, Michelle, so he turned to alcohol and sex to medicate his pain, and he gave in to the temptations that his coworker Leslie presented to him. He has now placed his entire homelife in harm's way, because he allowed his spirit to become indebted as well as his emotions. Satan used sex to control John. John was indebted to sex, and his relationship with sex caused him to suspend his morals, values, family, and friends. John sacrificed his marriage just so he could please what controlled him. Ask yourself: Who or what is controlling you?

We also create emotional debt when we carry grudges, envy, jealousy, or guilt around in our minds over things that have occurred in the past. When you hold on to issues that occurred in the past, those issues begin to weigh you down mentally and emotionally like a five-hundred-pound weight. Many of us look back on bad situations and replay them in our minds over and over like a bad movie. It's totally natural for us to reflect on things that have had an impact on us, but some people do not allow themselves to move forward emotionally from those situations.

Yes, there are many disappointing things that we go through that are very difficult to move past, such as a cheating spouse, betrayal by a close loved one, or even a traumatic experience such as fighting in a war. We, the authors, have had many friends who were military combat soldiers, who, unfortunately, were a part of wars during their time of service. These men and women experienced tremendous emotional distress, and at times they have found themselves weeping uncontrollably as they painfully relive the disastrous events of their past. If deliverance is not achieved, many who have had traumatic experiences may eventually lose themselves within their minds and become mentally and emotionally disturbed.

When this occurs, the doctors will then prescribe more medications to intoxicate the mind and subdue the emotions. This causes a vicious cycle of control that the enemy counts on to do his dirty deeds and create a sense of emotional indebtedness. Once he gets us trapped in this psychological prison, he tries to keep us there by constantly reminding us of the pain of our failures and disappointments. He keeps the automatic replay button on as a means of mind control and wants us to lose all hope. Satan will then tell us things such as "You are worthless," "Just give up," or "Nobody cares about you anyway."

He will relentlessly work on you psychologically until he breaks you down. After he breaks you, he will try to convince you to stop believing, stop trying, stop hoping, and ultimately stop living. This is why the suicide rates worldwide have increased to all-time highs. Do not allow him to put you into emotional indebtedness, because it's a matter of life and death.

One of the most powerful weapons the enemy uses against you in setting you up for emotional indebtedness is fear. Fear is a debilitating spirit and emotion that, throughout history, has caused more death, complacency, paranoia, and hopelessness than any other emotion we can imagine. The enemy has used fear tactics to get us to lose many battles in our lives and uses this emotion to lead us into making bad, life-altering decisions.

There are many types of fear: fear of failure, fear of success, fear of the unknown, fear of the dark, fear of heights, fear of small places; the list goes on. This by far is one of the enemy's best and most effective tools in keeping us in emotional debt.

The word of God teaches us in 2 Timothy 1:7, "God has not given us a spirit of fear, but of power, love, and a sound mind." Notice how the scripture teaches us that the opposite of a fearful mind is a sound mind. Therefore, when we are fearful, our minds are psychologically unsound or unstable. This obviously means that if our minds are unsound, then we cannot make sound decisions when we are under the influence of fear.

In times of fear, we must activate our faith in God and trust Him at His word. In the most notable Twenty-Third Psalm, God's word reads, "even though I walk through the valley of the shadow of death, I will fear no evil. For you are with me, your rod and staff comforts me."

When we become fearful, we need immediate comfort and reassurance that everything will be all right. God reassures us throughout his word that He is always with us, and we should not allow fear to overtake us. Fear is the ultimate threat to our faith. It will cause us to doubt and second guess our faith. Fear is an emotional cancer that drives us to be unproductive and ineffective.

Everyone experiences fear, including our Savior when He was about to go through His passion. When we read the scripture, we see that He prayed to the Father at least three times when preparing Himself to be crucified. In His prayers He asked the Father if there was any way that this cup could pass from Him. In other words He asked the Father if there was any other way to redeem us other than this excruciating passion experience. But in the end of His prayers Jesus says nevertheless, "Not my will, but let thy will be done."

You see, even though all flesh has experienced fear, our faith in God brings out our courage. Courage does not mean the absence of fear, but it means that we move forward with God's plan for our lives in spite of our fears. This is because our belief in the power of God overrides the fear that is designed to stop our victories. Just as Jesus faced His fears head on with prayer, so should we. When He prayed about His circumstance to the Father, He was then reassured of His mission and what He had to do. Jesus did not allow the emotion of fear to dictate His purpose, and neither should we. Jesus knew that the debt of sin had to be paid, and He was the only one in existence that could do it. Otherwise we all would have been lost for eternity. If Jesus had not gone through His passion, then all of our debts of sin, shame, guilt, oppression, and death would have still remained as a bounty on our heads.

Now that we know how we find ourselves in emotional debt, we must do what it takes to divorce it. Just as Jesus prayed to the Father for the strength and courage to go through with His mission and purpose, we must follow and do the same when we have emotional debt that we are holding on to. You see, Jesus gave His situation over to the Father in prayer, and His unwavering faith propelled Him to complete His task. We must cast our cares on Him in order to divorce our emotional debts. Once we do this, God responds by adding our emotional debts to the divorce decree in the spirit, and we become completely free to experience the godly emotions such as love, joy, compassion, excitement, and peace. Jesus is the Prince of Peace, and we are His heirs. Therefore, to have this peace, we must be free from all emotional debt that disrupts our faith and fellowship with God.

If we operate in true faith, which means that we fully trust in and believe God at His word, then we should not allow our temple to be exposed to lifestyles that bring forth contamination and defilement.

CHAPTER 5

Lifestyle Debt

There are countless lifestyle choices that we make each and every day. Some lifestyles may be worldlier in nature, while others may be more religious. Some of us surround ourselves with positive and productive influences, while others choose to immerse themselves in more destructive environments.

All in all, lifestyles are, for the most part, choices we make concerning our habits, our education, our community, the company we keep, the way in which we live, our religious beliefs, and our financial decisions.

Our lifestyle choices are a critical part of our discussion in this book, because they can determine what influences we are introducing ourselves to spiritually, emotionally, and financially.

If we are living a careless lifestyle and are not making wise decisions, then we set ourselves up to become a victim to the third type of debt: lifestyle debt. Lifestyle debt means we have surrendered our life to sin, which can lead to a lifestyle of iniquity. For the most part, our lifestyles choices are heavily influenced by the environments we grow up in. For example, if we grew up in a household where there was a spirit of ambition, success, and independence taught to us, then we will tend to live our lives in a manner that reflects this upbringing. Many times we judge our lifestyle choices by what our parents may have done in the past, which often has a tremendous influence on us.

Usually those who grow up in financially well-to-do households tend to shape or pattern their lifestyles around what they have become accustomed to. In contrast, those who grow up in chaos, confusion, and overall dysfunction may carry on dysfunction in their lifestyle decisions. People who grow up around drugs or alcohol may turn around and live a lifestyle that repeats this vicious cycle.

For example, part of why John, in our earlier example, was a salesperson was because his father was one when he was younger. So John witnessed his father's occupation and therefore wanted to be like him. These types of positive role model influences are actually a good thing for us when it comes to developing a good work ethic. However, on the flip side of things, although John's father helped to instill a positive career lifestyle characteristic in him, his father also presented a negative example by committing adultery against John's mother. When John was younger, he witnessed his father hanging out with his coworkers from time to time, and sometimes he did not see his father come home until the wee hours of the morning. He recalls that there were occasions where his father's infidelity was exposed through unexpected confrontations by other women who called their home, or even told neighbors about their affair, causing major conflict between his parents.

John vowed to himself at an early age that he would never treat his wife in such a manner. However, even though John tried to uphold his vow as a loyal husband and father, when the spiritual and emotional influences of life kicked in, he gave in to a lifestyle debt that was created in him by what he witnessed long ago in his father.

You see, because John's father made some very critical lifestyle decisions in the past, it gave John a subliminal reference point in starting down his path of adultery. John unconsciously opened himself and his family to a life of lies, deceit, distrust, and disloyalty. The problem with John's situation, for example, is that when the damage that he has caused with this extramarital relationship is revealed, he, as so many of us do, will try to place the blame on his father. Yes, our family and community influences can plant lifestyle seeds that can come out in negative ways at some point. However, we must not attempt to place blame on anyone for the choices we make.

As many of us do when we begin to develop bad and unhealthy relationships with lifestyle habits such as cheating, we will continue on this dark path until we are made aware of the impact of it. The enemy will oftentimes use our parents, siblings, friends, coworkers and so many other influences we are involved with to introduce us to destructive lifestyle paths. It is up to us to know what is right according to God's will and make righteous choices in our lives.

Our lifestyles must reflect our faith, and this cannot be taken for granted. You see, living a godly lifestyle is one of the highest forms of worship. The word states, "...they that worship the Lord must worship Him in Spirit and in Truth." This means that we must worship Him in the manner in which Jesus commands us. Jesus commands that we follow His lifestyle examples. We are in this world but not of this world, which means that there have to be limitations on the lifestyle activities and choices we make on a regular basis. To worship God is a lifestyle choice. Worship is not just limited to singing, praying, and praising God, as some in the body of Christ will lead us to believe. True worship penetrates our every lifestyle decision.

As an example of true worship, imagine having a newborn baby, but the catch to this scenario is that you have one main rule. The one rule you must follow is that you have to carry this baby in your arms twenty-four hours a day; you cannot put it down. Wherever you go, the baby must be in your arms. Whatever you do throughout the day, the baby must remain in your arms, depending on you for everything. How would your lifestyle decisions change if you had to do this for this baby? You would certainly think twice about every move you made, because you wouldn't want to hurt or harm this precious child. You would certainly not go rushing out the door to go to work, because you would want to make sure you don't drop the baby. You would almost certainly have to alter your normal travel routines as driving would probably not be an option since you could not put the baby down. You would be careful not to yell or be overly aggressive while the baby is asleep, because you don't want to disturb its peace and tranquility. Your level of patience and tolerance of those around you would certainly change, because everything becomes a matter of the baby's well-being.

Can you see where this is going? When we are in true worship with God, it is just like carrying the baby around with us 24-7. Our relationship of faith and worship impacts our lifestyle decisions on every level, and that is the true remedy for our lifestyle debt. When we take the focus off what we selfishly want for ourselves and allow God's will for us to be more precious to us, then we break free from the lifestyle bondage that the enemy wants to keep us entangled in.

God's word teaches us that our bodies are His temple and that the temple of God should never be defiled. If we operate in true faith, which means that we fully trust in and believe God at His word, then we should not allow our temple to be exposed to lifestyles that bring forth contamination and defilement.

If we are living in adultery, fornication, drunkenness, laziness, deceit, idolatry, lies, drug addiction, homosexuality, prostitution, arrogance, and so many other lifestyles, we are not worshipping God in holiness. If we are not worshipping God in holiness, how can we ever expect Him to help us divorce our debt?

The hardest thing to do for many people is to let go of something that they have become used to and are comfortable with. Often we hear people state that they will keep an old pair of shoes because they are comfortable, no matter how bad the condition of those shoes. Unfortunately, this is how some of us treat our bad habits and lifestyles; we feel that we might as well keep them in our lives, because they are comfortable.

God commands us to let it all go. Anything that hinders our worship of Christ must be let go. God's word states that we should have no other gods before Him.

In Matthew 19, Jesus encountered a rich young ruler who asked Him what he must do to be saved. Jesus told him to sell all his earthly goods, give the money to the poor, and follow Him. This rich young ruler was so caught up in his riches that he missed the opportunity to inherit a much greater possession: eternal life. This ruler was unwilling to give up what he perceived to be his most valuable possessions and did not realize that he was, in fact, in bondage to them. His lifestyle was dictated by his wealth, and he could not even see that he was actually in a major debt crisis.

You see, the more the world gives you, the more you owe the world. That's the whole point of this book. The world gives you false promises of happiness and joy but this is a major setup for enslavement. Nothing in the carnal world comes to us for free.

For example, if you gain a high political position, then you may have had to compromise many of your basic principles and integrity to get it. If so, your "lifestyle creditors" will always make sure you remember how much you owe them as you ascend to the top of the ladder. This type of debt or owing others will no doubt influence many of your decisions in an effort to hold on to your present lifestyle.

Jesus has always commanded us to let go of the world, separate ourselves from it, and follow Him. For those who choose wisely to let it all go and divorce their ungodly lifestyles, and the other debts previously discussed, there is a reward that is unmatched by anything we could ever experience.

We are called to live a holy lifestyle, according to Romans 12:1–2, and to be transformed by the renewing of our minds. This is the expectation of God for our lives, and in order to please Him, we must take action to divorce our lifestyle debts immediately.

If the world we live in can convince us to borrow money we do not have and purchase things we may not need on credit, then it can keep us busy working for the rest of our lives to pay it all off, knowing that many of us may never be able to do it.

CHAPTER 6

Financial Debt

In our previous chapters we have discussed and examined the dynamics of spiritual, emotional, and lifestyle debt. This final type of debt is one that we most readily identify with and recognize: financial debt. You see, this debt is really a culmination of the previous three. Many of us who end up over our heads in financial debt are there due to the impact of the previously mentioned debts we struggle with.

In other words, our finances are often out of sorts because we have made decisions on a spiritual, emotional, or lifestyle basis. The Bible teaches us the principles of good stewardship, and God expects us to make good decisions as they relate to our finances. This is an area that we, the authors, have had to deal with the most.

Financial debt is the new form of human slavery. The enemy figured it all out a long time ago. If the world we live in can convince us to borrow money we do not have and purchase things we may not need on credit, then it can keep us busy working for the rest of our lives to pay it all off, knowing that many of us may never be able to do it.

This evil system also knows debt will take us away from our families, our relationships, and ultimately God Himself. Satan knows that the more financial debt he can convince us to get ourselves into, the less time we will have to develop and strengthen our homes, our marriages, our positive relationships, and our faith. When financial debt is growing rapidly in our lives, it takes our attention off of the things that matter the most, and Satan knows this all too well. When we see ourselves getting into debt, we must remember this acronym for it; debt stands for the **DE**vil's **B**est **T**rap. A trap represents bondage.

Financial responsibility is not taught in many households or schools, and some children grow up with the notion that whenever they receive any financial resources, it is their right to spend it on things that are unnecessary. Many years ago, our parents and grandparents practiced the rule that if you don't have the money to buy something in cash, then don't get it. This fundamental concept is one that should have remained as a part of basic home training and culture. This is a principle that should also be taught in every school in the world.

We, the authors, have attended grammar school, high school, and college. We did not see then and have yet to see a course crafted to promote financial responsibility. This is probably because the world is designed to keep us ignorant to true financial stewardship, financial literacy, and responsibility. Most people do not know that this world's financial system is built on debt. Yes, this is how so many companies and individuals become so successful in such a short period of time. Our financial system was crafted to allow our government and businesses to expand in rapid financial growth through debt creation.

This is how it works: The Federal Reserve Bank lends money to the federal government and to the nation's banks so that loans and investments can be made. These loans have a wholesale interest rate attached to them. Let's say, for example purposes, that the interest rate is 1 percent. This means that the banks and the US government must pay back every dollar it borrows from the Federal Reserve Bank and pay it back with 1 percent interest on top.

The banks and the government take this money and lend it out to businesses, homeowners, and personal credit borrowers at a higher interest rate. So for example, the bank borrowed the money from the Federal Reserve at a 1 percent wholesale rate, and it then lends you some of that money at a 5 percent retail rate. Now the bank is expecting you to not only pay them back the principal amount you borrowed, but they expect your interest payments to pay the interest they owe to the Federal Reserve and make the bank a profit on top of that.

When the government borrows money from the Federal Reserve, it also makes loans to other countries and invests it in various interest-earning opportunities. This allows the government to use its investment earnings to offset the amount of money that has to be paid back to the Federal Reserve.

The government also has another major way that it pays back the debts it owes to the Federal Reserve and others. The government charges working citizens income tax on all wages, which is collected by the Internal Revenue Service (IRS). The IRS collects the taxpayer dollars and pays down the government's debt with a good portion of this money collected. The money from tax collection will also be used to pay the internal bills of the government such as payroll and other ongoing expenses. When money collection is too low to cover expenses, the government will find ways to increase our taxes.

Many of us have heard the term "deficit spending" by the government, which is really another way of saying spending money we really don't have! We have all been conditioned to emulate the patterns of the government and business community and spend money we don't have. This is why credit cards are so plentiful and so easy to get. The credit card system is designed and engineered to keep us in this perpetual pattern of financial slavery. Because the word of God teaches us that the borrower is a slave to the lender, the more debt you owe, the more of a slave you become.

Let's just take a look a moment at the wording of some of the credit card companies. "MasterCard" is the label that expresses exactly what we are discussing here in this chapter. This company is letting us know that they seek to be our master if we do business with them.

Visa means "permitting entry into and travel within a particular country or region." Notice how this definition has the word permitting in it. This indicates another controlling power that gives us permission to move about in the world. If you must seek permission, than you are under the control of someone or something, i.e., a master.

Finally, as we previously mentioned in chapter 3, the word "mortgage" is something that every homeowner is quite familiar with. What most people do not know is that the word "mortgage" actually means "death pledge." When we look up the historical origins of this word, we find that "mort" means death and "gage" means pledge. So guess what, when you sign on the dotted line for the American dream of homeownership, you are actually making an agreement that indicates you will probably die trying to pay for this debt. Why do we think most mortgages go out for thirty years or even more these days? Many homeowners will be seduced into doing a refinance with promises of a lower payment, not realizing that if they sign up for another thirty years, they have just renewed that death pledge.

This type of information was astounding to us, the authors, when we learned about it, because it really confirms what the word of God has warned us about in so many scriptures. The word teaches us that we are to obey those who have rule over us, so when we sign on to go into debt with the credit card, finance, and mortgage companies, we are essentially placing ourselves into voluntary slavery. We have all been brainwashed by this system of credit, and our goal is to make sure you wake up from your sleep and free yourself from this oppressive and evil system.

When we are not good stewards over our money, Satan comes in to tempt us to borrow, borrow, borrow, spend, spend, and spend—largely what we do not have. He knows that once the debts have mounted, he can then force us unknowingly into a slavery state of mind and living.

The Bible teaches us in Proverbs 22:7 that "the rich rule over the poor and the borrower is a servant to the lender." The Bible also teaches us in Romans 13:8 that we are not to owe any man anything except love. These are Kingdom principles of financial living. The enemy wants you to live in his world of slavery and financial destruction so he can control your worship and praise.

God however, wants us to live in godly financial stewardship. The following list outlines the ten basic godly financial principles that we should live by in our finances:

1. **Pray over your finances daily.**

   Don't worry about anything; instead, pray about everything (Phil 4:6, NLT).

   And we are confident that he hears us whenever we ask for anything that pleases Him (1 John 5:14, NLT).

This step is the most important part of every aspect of our lives, and it opens the door to the power of God. God's word is filled with scriptures on the power of prayer, but many of us neglect to pray over our finances. It seems that we are willing to pray over everything else in our lives except this area. Is it because some of our spiritual leaders have made some of us feel guilty about having money? Is it because some leaders have talked so much about prosperity that it has turned us off from wanting to have sufficient financial resources?

Perhaps it is a combination of these types of things. The bottom line, however, is that we should offer up prayer for our ability to manage our finances wisely and to be good stewards over them. We, the authors, are firm believers that in all things, prayer is in order. According to God's word, God knows all too well what we are in need of even before we ask, so to neglect prayer in all our needs, including our finances, would be foolish.

From our perspective, we believe we should pray that God will provide for our daily and future financial needs. If we are bad with money, we should pray that God will improve our ability to manage it better or help us meet someone who can assist us in managing our finances.

Everyone should seek out sound financial expertise from a professional who can counsel you on sound money management. I, Terrence Trimuel, Sr., became a financial adviser in 2001, because I recognized my own shortcomings with money management and wanted to make sure that I learned how money really worked. Because I had made so many errors in my own finances, and I saw so many people making the same or worse mistakes around me, I decided to learn the system of money management and investments. This decision was not just for my family and me but to help others in our lives understand the principles that could save them financially, which so many of the wealthy are taught early in life.

There are many families and individuals who never learn anything about money management except how to open a checking and savings account. Beyond that, much of our society has no real clue as to how to properly manage its finances. This, again, is by design. The enemy knows all too well that if he can keep you ignorant and constantly tempted to squander your financial resources, he can eventually gain control over your life through financial debt.

At some point you will have to borrow money or rob Peter to pay Paul just to survive. This is why we must start to pray over our finances: so God will release His holy wisdom and lead us in sound financial stewardship.

2. **Work an honest job or run an honest business for your living.**

   .... Wealth from get-rich-quick schemes quickly disappears; wealth from hard work grows (Proverbs 13:11).

> *We hear that some of you are living idle lives, refusing to work and wasting time meddling in other people's business. In the name of the Lord Jesus Christ, we appeal to such people—no, we command them: Settle down and get to work. Earn your own living (2 Thessalonians 3:11–12).*

> *Begin using your hands for honest work, and then give generously to others in need (Ephesians 4:28).*

There are so many people who have been deceived in our world by promises of wealth by illegal or unprofitable means. When we take a look at many of our urban areas, we see an alarming level of drugs, prostitution, and gambling being glorified in the eyes of our youth as the way to get what they want. This trick of Satan has been tearing down families and communities for far too long.

The enemy will take men and women who have decided to "hustle for the money" and promote their perceived successes with lavish cars, money, clothing, jewelry, and other material goods. Young children are extremely impressionable, so once these images of drug dealers, prostitutes, and hustlers are reinforced over and over again in their communities, they believe that in order to live "the good life," they must follow these bad examples.

Living in many of these communities is very similar to the wilderness experience that Jesus went through right before He began His ministry. God led His son Jesus into the wilderness right after His baptism to be tempted by the devil right before He was to begin to teach and preach. Satan, however, approached Jesus at the end of His fasting period of forty days and forty nights to attempt to get Him to abandon His Holy mission so He could obtain things that would please His flesh.

In this story, one thing we notice is that Satan waited until Jesus suffered through hunger so long to bring forth his temptations and attack. He thought by catching Jesus at His weakest physical point, he could get Jesus to break His commitment to God and destroy the plan of salvation. We all know who won that battle, of course, but this illustrates to us just how the enemy works to get us to do things the easy way.

You see, just as Satan came to Jesus at His time of hunger and weakness, he comes to us in those same moments of weakness and hunger. Many young people are living without one or both parents. In most cases, the parent who is missing is the father, who represents authority. When parents are struggling to make ends meet and are unable to adequately provide for the children, the hunger for a better life sets in and makes these young people yearn for more.

This yearning then signals the enemy to present them with an alternative that takes them down a road of destruction and sin. You see, to pursue financial success through illegal and unlawful means sets you up for a major failure or fall that sometimes cannot be reversed. When our young people get wrapped up in illegal or frivolous means of obtaining money, they sell themselves into financial debt or slavery, because they enter a world that requires their lives in order to get out. The word of God teaches us in Mark 8:36, "For what shall it profit a man, if he shall gain the whole world, and lose his own soul?"

We must not involve ourselves in quick money-making schemes or hustles if we want God to bless us and keep ourselves from an even worse kind of financial debt.

God wants us to work for an honest living—one that reflects integrity and allows us to sleep peacefully at night. This is why we must go through a season of preparation. This is usually what we call education.

Education is important, because it sets the stage for our success in earning an honest living. We all know that not everyone is cut out for college. There are many people who are better at jobs and roles that do not require a college education. We, the authors, agree that not everyone can go to an institution of higher learning, but we believe that we all should never stop learning. Learning new things and better ways of doing things should always be a part of our lives. Learning keeps us prepared for any unforeseen circumstances that may arise at our jobs, so we can be prepared to do something else.

When we bring knowledge together with wisdom and understanding, we can take on those jobs or business opportunities that will bring us long-term prosperity. This is what God expects from us.

3. **When you get paid, always pay God His money first in the form of tithes and offerings, and He will bless you immensely!**

   Will a man rob God? Yet ye have robbed me. But ye say, wherein have we robbed thee? In tithes and offerings. Ye are cursed with a curse: for ye have robbed me, even this whole nation. Bring all the tithes into the storehouse so there will be enough food in my Temple. If you do, I will open the win-

> *dows of heaven for you. I will pour out a blessing so great you won't have enough room to take it in! Try it! Let me prove it to you! (Malachi 3:8–10)*
> *Honor the Lord with your wealth and with the best part of everything you produce. Then he will fill your barns with grain, and your vats will overflow with good wine (Proverbs 3:9–10).*

This is a spiritual principle that cannot be overstated. The word teaches us that we rob God when we do not give our tithes and offerings. Robbery is a crime, according to the law of the land. To rob someone is actually a different crime than burglary/stealing. Most people never take the time to learn the distinct difference. When you are "burglarized," someone steals something from you, usually while you are not present, or you never see it occur. However when someone "robs" you, they take by force from you what belongs to you, usually in plain sight.

God is teaching us through His word that when we withhold our tithes and offerings, we are taking from

Him what rightfully belongs to Him. When we do this, we are bringing a curse over our finances and other resources, which may cause lack in many areas of our lives. He's telling us to repent and bring His portion of our finances and resources to the storehouse so that others will be taken care of. He also challenges us to test Him on this to prove that He will bless us.

What God is trying to get us to see is that God's 10 percent blesses and sanctifies the 90 percent of our resources. When we take God's portion off the top of our financial increase, we make a spiritual deposit in the Holy Bank of God that releases His blessings upon whatever we do or touch. God does not want us to suffer, so He lays out His expectations of how we are to handle our finances and His. Financial debt is a curse, and God wants us to avoid being under this curse at all costs.

When we give God His tithes and offerings willingly, we affirm our commitment to His covenant with us in the area of our finances. Our finances can remain in a blessed state if we just obey God's mandate to give what is required of us. To take this lightly is a grave mistake, and it is a major reason why so many people struggle with their finances.

4. **Pay yourself next by putting a portion of your income in a savings or some sort of interest-bearing account.**
   You who have been faithful over a few things; I will put you in charge of many things (Matthew 25: 23).

One phrase that I, Terrence Trimuel, Sr., learned early in my career as a financial professional that has always stuck with me is: "Those who understand interest, collect it, those who don't, pay it." As a financial professional, I have had the privilege to work with many clients in this area of discussion. It is important that we all have a personal financial game plan to help us prepare for the future. This game plan should include saving a portion of our money in an interest-bearing account. There are many types of accounts out there.

However, probably the most familiar one is a savings account.

Usually a savings account is set up for short-term and midterm goals and emergencies. We should all have some sort of interest-bearing account to provide us with funds for that rainy day or emergency. One thing for sure is that life happens, and when it does, each one of us should have an emergency fund that we can have easy and quick access to. At the same time, we want this account to be earning interest. As you earn interest, your money is accumulating more money that you don't have to work for. This is one of the most important principles of building and sustaining personal wealth. Always earn more interest than you pay.

Savings accounts usually provide you with a very small amount of interest on your money, so this kind of account should not be used as a retirement account. Savings accounts are usually geared to provide you with an account that you can easily get to quickly, yet also allow you to earn some small portion of interest.

A savings account can be established at your current or local banking institution. If you are working with a financial consultant, however, it is also a good idea to seek guidance from that person as to where you should establish your savings account. Financial consultants usually can open an account for you to fulfill this need.

Remember that a savings account should be used primarily for immediate financial emergencies and short-term financial goals, such as paying off certain bills.

5. **Invest a portion of your income for the future in retirement accounts, mutual funds, or some form of investment account that provides growth potential for the long-term.**

   He called together his servants and gave them money to invest for him while he was gone (Matthew 25:14).

Those who understand the importance of saving for retirement should be looking at accounts that are specifically designed for retirement such as 401k, IRA, or a 403b accounts. These kinds of accounts are usually designed to provide you with more interest-earning potential over time.

We all age, and most of us will come to a time when we cannot work any longer to support ourselves. When this happens, we call this retirement.

Back in the days of our parents and grandparents, the US Social Security system would provide retirees with some level of financial support when they retired. In today's world, this kind of financial support is all but dwindling away. The system that was once considered a guaranteed safety net for the retired elderly is now looking like a fleeting fantasy in the eyes of the future retirees of our country.

The rule of seventy-two is something that all of the children in school should be taught. This rule has been tested over time and has proved to be a stellar principle in planning for retirement. This means that this rule is important to remember, so please take note. The rule of seventy-two teaches us that if you take the number seventy-two and divide it by the interest rate you expect to receive over time, it will tell you how many years it will take for your money to double. So for example if you want to earn a rate of return of 10 percent, your investment would take 7.2 years to double.

$$72/10 = 7.2$$

This means that the money you have invested would double every 7.2 years at a 10 percent rate of return.

Initial investment	= $10,000
Year 7	= $20,000
Year 14	= $40,000
Year 21	= $80,000
Year 28	= $160,000

As you can see, over the years a small investment can turn into a large nest egg for retirement. And this is assuming only the initial investment of $10,000. It is not including additional retirement contributions. Imagine how this could grow when you add consistently to your retirement plan.

Time is your best friend when you are saving for retirement. The earlier you start a retirement account, such as a 401K, 403B, or an IRA, the better your chances of accumulating a substantial nest egg for retirement. If you start in your early twenties, for example, and you continue to make systematic contributions from each paycheck over thirty years, it is very likely you may actually have over a million dollars to retire on. This is, of course, assuming you have a game plan and a qualified professional to coach you along the way. It also depends on how disciplined and diversified you're able to be with your plan. In other words, you must stay committed to investing consistently in your retirement accounts in order for them to pay off when you need them.

So many of the wealthy in our world were taught this very simple yet valuable principle at an early age. This is a part of the key to the wealthy avoiding financial debt in their lives, while we suffer from a lack of knowledge. The word of God teaches us that His people are destroyed by a lack of knowledge. Make sure you seek out a financial professional who can further direct you in setting up a retirement account that is appropriate for you.

6. Create a realistic budget

> *For which of you, intending to build a tower, sitteth not down first, and counteth the cost, whether he have sufficient to finish it? Lest haply, after he hath laid the foundation, and is not able to finish it, all that behold it begin to mock him, saying, this man began to build, and was not able to finish (Luke 14:28–30).*

So many of us are reluctant to take this very critical step in developing a budget and more important, sticking to it. In my career as a financial services professional, I have heard many excuses for why people do not want to create a budget. Out of all the reasons people have told me, the most common excuse is that a budget is too restrictive and too much like being in financial prison.

Of course, this is not true at all as it relates to creating a budget. The enemy is very crafty and tries to convince us that having and maintaining a budget is going to hurt our financial freedom, but this couldn't be further from the truth. A budget is not synonymous with bondage. In fact, a properly crafted budget can give you a better sense of freedom and responsibility.

What most people do not realize is that when a budget is created properly, in addition to planning out the money that will be spent on necessary bills, it also includes the amount of your money that can be spent on things you want to have fun with. When you are able to know up front at the beginning of the week or month what exactly you can afford to spend on entertainment or self-indulgences, it actually helps you avoid getting into financial bondage. This is because you will usually make better decisions and time when those decisions will be made so that you are in control, not out of control. Usually a person without a budget is actually out of control of his or her finances and spending habits. If you live an out of control lifestyle, it will almost always lead you to bondage at some point.

I think most of us do not want to create a budget, because it forces us to be accountable for our spending habits and to create a disciplined approach to our finances. In the previous scripture, found in Luke 14, Jesus is using a parable to illustrate the importance of wisdom in planning for those things that are important in life. Without a budget, we risk depending on our own restraint and memory to keep our spending habits in check. Emotional debt makes us make irrational decisions. Many of those decisions involve unwisely spending our money on things we don't need or at the wrong time. Emotional debt can then lead us not only into lifestyle debt, but also financial debt.

When you create a budget, it's a good idea to seek professional assistance from a financial planner or consultant. This will help you avoid leaving out crucial parts of a budget that can be easily overlooked. Every part of your budget is important, including the personal spending allowances. Your budget should always be realistic, based on the actual dollars you bring in, and not based on anticipated finances. Keep in mind that a budget is not set in stone, so you should always allow for miscellaneous and unexpected things to come up.

If your finances increase or decrease, you should immediately adjust your budget, so it always reflects the true nature of your financial situation.

Don't be afraid of sitting down and tracking your expenditures. This will allow you to face the truth about where your money is going and help you start the process of deliverance from out-of-control spending habits.

7. Pay your bills and debts on time whenever possible, and pay off all debt as soon as possible.

Just as the rich rule the poor, so the borrower is servant to the lender (Proverbs 22:7).

Pay your taxes, too, for these same reasons. For government workers need to be paid. They are serving God in what they do. Give to everyone what you owe them: Pay your taxes and government fees to those who collect them, and give respect and honor to those who are in authority. Owe nothing to anyone—except for your obligation to love one another (Romans 13:6–8).

This sounds self explanatory. However, there are many people who are chronically late paying their bills on time. We, the authors, must admit that we too struggle in this area at times, and this is something we have to constantly work on to improve. What you must realize is that whenever you have bills that you don't pay on time, you may actually damage your credit and budget plan, because most companies, agencies, and utilities charge us late fees and additional interest when we are late.

This means that if you bought $20 worth of groceries on a credit card but failed to pay your monthly bill on time, you may actually end up paying $30 or $40 for those same groceries when you finally pay the late fees, penalties, and extra interest. This can really add up if you are a chronic late payer and cause you to go deeper into unnecessary financial bondage. Sometimes, as we know, life happens, and we cannot always pay our bills on time. However, there are many among us who have the ability and financial means to pay our bills on time, but because of our slothful attitude, we fail to execute the good stewardship God requires of us.

Another secret that most creditors won't tell you is that not only should you pay on time, but you should pay more than your minimum amount due if you are paying on an account that accrues interest. This is because the sooner you pay it off, the more money you save. You could literally save thousands of dollars in interest payments when you pay more than the minimum amounts due.

In other words, the faster you pay the debt, the faster you come out of bondage.

Every one of us should develop a game plan to attack and destroy our debts. After all, this is at the core of what this book is all about. When you sit down with a good financial consultant, you should always make a plan to eliminate your debt as quickly as possible.

"And if that happens, you surely won't be free again until you have paid the last penny."
(Matthew 5:26 NLT)

Although there are many strategies to accomplish this goal, there is one method in particular that I prefer.

This method is called debt stacking. Debt stacking is a technique where you arrange all of your consumer debts such as car notes, credit cards, lines of credit, mortgages, and any other interest-accruing debt from the smallest balance to the largest.

You can simply write them on some paper at the kitchen table if you want, or do a computer spreadsheet. Once you have them organized from the smallest balance to the largest, you then determine how much extra you can afford to pay monthly on the smallest bill to pay it off more quickly. Once that bill has been paid off, you then take the same total money that went toward that first bill, including the extra money, and apply it to the next bill in line until it is paid off. By doing this, you are increasing the monthly payment substantially and are accelerating the payoff of all your debts. You are thus saving yourself thousands of dollars of interest and debt bondage.

On the next page is an example of how this plan might look to accelerate the divorce of your financial debt.

CREDIT TYPE	BALANCE	MIN. PAYMENT	ACCELERATED
Credit card 1	$500	$20 (+$30 extra)	$50 (Including $30 extra until paid off)
Credit card 2	$1,000	$50	$100 (After credit card 1 is paid off)
Line of credit	$2,500	$100	$200 (After credit card 2 is paid off)
Car note	$15,000	$450	$650 (After line of credit is paid off)
Mortgage	$100,000	$850	$1,500 (After car note is paid off)
Totals	**$119,000**	**$1,470**	

With this strategy, you will be able to eliminate your debt more quickly than by just paying the monthly minimum amount. You are able to accomplish this by starting with an extra $30 on your first bill until it is paid off. The key to this strategy being truly effective, however, is your ability and discipline to stay away from adding new debts while going through this process. That, of course, is the challenge.

8. **Purchase only the things you need, and don't use credit cards to get them.**

> *Do not be a man who strikes hands in pledge or puts up security for debts; if you lack the means to pay, your very bed will be snatched from under you (Proverbs 22:26–27).*

This is a concept that has been lost and all but forgotten. Years ago, our parents and grandparents practiced this general rule, and even though they may not have made a lot of money from their occupations, they always knew that it was dangerous to purchase something without having the money up front.

The enemy has come along in today's world and has made credit easy to get from just about every finance company, store, or retail business that you can imagine. Of course, this makes getting into financial debt so much easier than ever before. Today you don't even have to request an application because the invitation to obtain credit is always in your mailbox. All you have to do is call in to a number or log onto the website of the solicitor, and within moments, voila! You have credit! It's easy to get in debt, but ten times more difficult to get out. This is how the enemy uses temptation to lure us into voluntary submission.

That's how bondage works. It is so easy to get into bondage, but it is often the hardest thing in the world to escape. When you want something that can wait, and you do not have the funds at the time to buy it in cash, please, please, please do not use your credit to purchase it. With the interest, it can cost you twice as much in the long run. That just creates an accident waiting to happen.

Instead, try to plan your purchases in advance as much as possible. If it's a larger-cost item, plan a savings strategy over time to purchase it. This is where that savings account mentioned earlier will come in handy. One key point to mention here is that when we work for the things in life we really want and don't get them so easily handed to us, we tend to appreciate them more because of what it took for us to get those things. These are principles we absolutely must teach our children and others to follow.

9. **Give a portion of your income to the poor and less fortunate. This principle really pleases God and will sow seeds of good harvest back to you a hundredfold.**

Whoever gives to the poor will lack nothing (Proverbs 28:27).

If you give, you will receive. Your gift will return to you in full measure…running over (Luke 6:38).

This is a spiritual law that cannot be overstated. When you give of yourself to others, God will bless you that others will give to you. God's word states that we are to give to the poor and less fortunate because they will be with us always. When we show this kind of compassion for people, God opens up the windows of heaven and allows blessings to flow back to us. Many of those blessings are financial.

All that we have comes from God, and he expects His good stewards to help those who cannot help themselves.

We are to make sure that when we receive financial blessings from God, that we show compassion for people who do not have the same means or financial status.

10. Last but not least; Each one teach one

> *Train up a child in the way he should go, and when he is old, he will not depart from it (Proverbs 22:6).*

When we know better, we are to do better, and we are to teach others the truth. When we experience deliverance from financial bondage, God wants us to share that freedom with others. The Bible states, "He whom the Son sets free is truly free indeed." We have to share our experiences and victories with others who may be experiencing the financial bondage we were delivered from. This is especially true with our children. God's word states that we are to "train up a child in the way he should go and when he is old, he will not depart from it."

Good sound training in finances is missing in today's world, and we must do what it takes to create an environment of learning for our children and others. When our children are taught the very critical lessons of financial stewardship, we can keep them out of the bondage that so many of us have experienced. This will help them to save their marriages and keep their families together. It can help keep them from opening doors to depression, anger, bitterness, rejection, addiction, and all-around hopelessness that so many people have fallen victim to and become enslaved by. As we witness the economic meltdown of our financial systems, the dire need to teach financial literacy cannot be overstated in today's culture. So many people lost their jobs, homes, families, and lives because they just were not properly prepared to deal with matters of finance. We must be vigilant in this crusade to teach people these fundamental lessons of money and stewardship, so the debts we all experience can be properly divorced.

God wants us to divorce our debts, because they truly hinder our ability to praise Him, worship Him, and live a life of peace and victory.

CHAPTER 7

The Final Divorce Decree
(It Is Finished)

This seventh and final chapter denotes completion as it represents such in the Holy Word. God created the world in six days, and on the seventh day, He rested. When we have had to battle with all the areas of debt—spiritual, emotional, lifestyle, and financial—for such a long time, our minds and bodies need rest.

Throughout this book we have discussed how each of the major forms of debt impacts our mind, body, soul, spirit, families, relationships, and lifestyles. Any relationship that causes us to be unhealthy, angry, stressed out, and oppressed has to be looked at and re-evaluated in order to make the changes necessary and bring forth peace. God's word teaches us that He is not the author of confusion, and our relationship with the areas of life that keep us in bondage is not of God. God wants us to divorce our debts, because they truly hinder our ability to praise Him, worship Him, and live a life of peace and victory. Jesus is known as the Prince of Peace and those who believe in Him have unlimited access to that peace.

The goal of the enemy is to kill, steal, and destroy us all, and one of the most powerful and effective weapons he has is debt. Remember, debt is bondage, and the whole nature of the enemy is to trap us and keep us trapped in bondage so that we cannot be free to worship, serve, and celebrate God in our lives. This was evident in the Exodus experience that the Israelites went through. Pharaoh kept them in bondage for hundreds of years and did not want to release them, even after Moses proved the power of God was with the Israelites. One key point that was repeated over and over by Moses to Pharaoh was that he must let go of God's people in order to go serve and worship Him. They could not serve Him and worship Him properly as long as they remained in the bondage of oppression that Pharaoh had them under. The same holds true for us today; we cannot serve and worship God properly as long as we are under bondage and oppression.

Once we recognize that we are in bondage, we must make the decision to break free from bondage. Some people have a hard time letting go of bad relationships, because they have become too comfortable and are too familiar to them. They allow the fear of the unknown to keep them entangled in unhealthy relationships, which in turn deprives them of so many of the promises of God. The longer we decide to stay in bondage, the longer we delay our blessings from the Lord.

You have the key to break free from every weight of bondage and debt that has set you back. All you must do is make a firm decision to divorce your debt. Now, we all know that divorces can be messy, daunting, and painful. Oftentimes people get caught up in paperwork, legal proceedings, and expensive attorney's fees, and by the time the divorce is over, they find some parts of their lives in a worse condition than they were before. Well, we thank God that even though the process for divorcing your debt can also be a tough one for many people, the difference is that you can do this divorce without an attorney, without the legal paperwork, without the costly financial burdens, and without the drama. All you have to do is to acknowledge the fact that it is time to make a serious change for your life and put your trust in the One who can change all your life circumstances.

He's better than any attorney and doesn't cost you a dime. He is always available when you call on Him, yet He has no phone number. He will be your best advocate as you fight through the process of debt deliverance. He will comfort you during the times when you question your new decision and seek to go back into bondage as a comfort zone. He will turn you around and redirect your life so that you can be free to worship, serve, and celebrate Him. His name is Jesus Christ, and He is hereby serving all your debts the official Kingdom Divorce Decree notice. This decree has outlined each part of your life from spiritual to financial and requires the immediate release, annulment, and dissolution of your marriage to your debts and bondage.

Divorce Your Debt

Kingdom Divorce Decree Dissolution of Debt:

~OFFICIAL NOTICE~

This decree hereby declares the complete and utter dissolution of marriage to all forms of spiritual, emotional, lifestyle, and financial debt that has been incurred by me.

This decree hereby establishes that I am completely set free from all oppression and bondage that has been placed on me involuntarily or by my own free will.

This decree declares that I acknowledge that I no longer have to accept the lies and deceit of the enemy, the father of lies.

This decree further declares that in the name of Jesus, each and every weight, cord of oppression, band, and yoke of debt are hereby cast down and destroyed in my life.

This decree hereby establishes that I have professed my faith in Christ and have hereby been adopted into His family, which thereby makes me an heir to the Kingdom. As an heir to the Kingdom, I have been granted peace, freedom, love, joy, patience, kindness, and eternal life that cannot and will not be revoked.

Furthermore, I declare that I am more than a conqueror, and greater is He who is within me, than he who is in the world. I have been given access to a more abundant life, and no weapon formed against me will prosper.

This decree grants me authority over every situation and circumstance that seeks to enslave me or place me back in bondage.

From this day forward, I will protect my spirit by continuously praying to the Lord, studying His word, and trusting Him in all things.

I will, from this day forward, disallow my emotions to lead me into the traps of bad decisions and bad relationships.

From this day forward, I will not allow my lifestyle to become one that hinders my holiness and worship unto God.

From this day forward, I will be a good steward over my finances and not allow my spiritual, emotional, and lifestyle debts to lead me into financial bondage.

I am hereby completely free and divorced from all of my debts, and I am hereby given back my true SELF in the name of Jesus. My new identity in Christ is now henceforth and forevermore recorded in the book of life and will be kept in the eternal archives of Heaven.

Peace and blessings be unto you.

I am hereby forgiven and will sin no more. Peace and blessings be unto me.

Signed by:

____

on this ________________ day in

the year of our Lord _________

Sealed by the Blood of Jesus
Witnessed by the Father,
Son, and Holy Spirit

*Forever, O LORD, your word
is settled in heaven
(Psalm 119:89).*

About the Authors

Don't copy the behavior and customs of this world, but let God transform you into a new person by changing the way you think. Then you will learn to know God's will for you, which is good and pleasing and perfect (Romans 12:2).

Terrence and Marlene Trimuel are in the ministry of transforming lives through books, trainings, seminars, and workshops. As transformational leaders, they have created holistic training programs that will allow individuals to grow in discipleship for Christ.

Their passion for teaching has allowed them to create seminars and workshops for spiritual and personal development that include marriage, finance, relationships, leadership, women, men, teens, and preaching the gospel to lost souls. They are also certified financial education instructors and believe in teaching Kingdom wealth and stewardship.

Divorce Your Debt was written to help the reader identify the key areas and situations in his or her life that represents bondage and debt. As individuals, we find ourselves getting involved in toxic relationships with people, things, bad habits, and our past experiences. After a while, we tend to become unconsciously "married" to these toxic relationships.

Divorce Your Debt is a spiritual, emotional, lifestyle, and financial **(SELF)** toxicology test. It will allow you to examine yourself and the unconscious toxic relationships you have formed in each of the four major areas of SELF.

Divorce Your Debt is a guide to wholeness. It's a declaration of independence and a decree to become free from "every weight that so easily besets us." It's a conscious choice to become liberated from the chains, bondage, and traps of the enemy. We all need to divorce or rid ourselves of something in our lives, so we can truly follow God's will and please the Master.

Divorce Your Debt will guide you from debt to deliverance so you can set your **SELF** free!